# GOING OUT OF BUSINESS SERIES

---

## VOLUME 1

# How Holy Is Matrimony?
*Rethinking the Church's Role in the Wedding Business*

## Amie Martin
*Foreword by Michael Adam Beck*

T0016872

The internet addresses, email addresses, and phone numbers in this book are accurate at the time of publication. They are provided as a resource. The author and publisher do not endorse them or vouch for their content or permanence.

HigherLife Development Services, Inc.
PO Box 623307
Oviedo, Florida 32762
(407) 563-4806
www.ahigherlife.com

Cover Design: Aspen D. Alva

Library of Congress Cataloging-in-Publication Data
A complete catalog record for this book is available from the Library of Congress.

ISBN: 979-8-9859212-8-1 (paperback)
ISBN: 979-8-9859212-9-8 (ebook)

Printed in the United States of America
10 9 8 7 6 5 4 3 2 1

# TABLE OF CONTENTS

# FOREWORD

Jesus wasn't big on what we might call "family values." On one occasion, Jesus is with his disciples teaching and his bio mom and siblings show up. Someone interrupts the moment, saying, "Your mother and brothers are standing outside, wanting to speak to you."

Jesus' reply almost seems shocking to our modern sensibilities, "Who is my mother, and who are my brothers?" Then he points to the disciples, and says, "Here are my mother and my brothers" (Matt 12:46-50). Jesus is highlighting the reality that the community of disciples, what would later be called the *church*, is a big, blended, messy family that includes everyone across every race, space, and time. Belonging to this family supersedes and would even cause division and strife in biological families (Matt 10:21). Indeed, following Jesus has caused alienation and exile in families for 2000 years.

The church is to be a community where we find healing from all life's traumas, including family wounds. Sadly, at times, people find the church to be more or equally dysfunctional than their family of origin.

So, it's interesting then that instructing people how to be a family in the "Christian way" has become big business for the church. Just think of the countless organizations, books, seminars, and gurus who generate incredible sums of income to give the secrets to success in building a "Christian family" or a "Christian marriage."

Can a family shattered by divorce or infidelity be a Christian family? Or is a family in which one parent is an active alcoholic, but attends church every Sunday a Christian family? What about some of the fastest growing family forms, single parent and blended families? Are they Christian too?

Jesus also wasn't big on our conventional understanding of marriage. The only wedding the Bible reports he attended was one in which he was on the guest list, not the officiant (Jn 2:1–11). Obviously, Jesus himself wasn't married.

In one of his more controversial teachings on the subject, he disrupts our modern sensibilities once again. A group of religious leaders show up, those who didn't believe in resurrection. They try to trap Jesus in a complicated hypothetical marriage situation. A woman marries a man with seven brothers. Each brother dies, passing on the widow to the next brother. In the patriarchal arranged marriage system prominently featured in the Bible, women were essentially property, with no real rights or protections against abuse.

Since in this case the woman had seven husbands, they asked, "In the resurrection, then, whose wife of the seven will she be? For all of them had married her." Jesus answered them, "You are wrong because you know neither the scriptures nor the power of God. For in the resurrection people neither marry nor are given in marriage but are like angels of God in heaven" (Matt 22:23-33).

Wait a minute, say what Jesus? What about the idea of soul mates and lifelong unions that endure for all eternity? Jesus doesn't seem to support the current expression of these ideas.

It's astonishing that the church has placed such an emphasis on marriage. Marriage in the church is big business. Again, think of all the organizations, seminars, books, and gurus selling products on how to build a "Christian marriage." Just consider how the church itself has been involved in selling our spaces and peddling clergy to officiate over these "holy unions," to make them "official."

There is not a single scriptural reference for a clergyperson to preside, officiate, sanction, give permission, or represent God in wedding ceremonies. When the church holds so much power and authority over weddings, many people become spiritually confused, asking questions such as: What about children whose lives are shattered by divorce? Was their parents' union holy for them? Or how about the good Christian wife who takes her beating from her abusive husband, night after night, because of a toxic and unbiblical theology around suffering well in holy matrimony? Or what about Christians of various sexual orientations who can't understand why their denominational home won't consider their lifelong, monogamous union holy?

Perhaps the most powerful image in Scripture regarding marriage is one in which the overarching metaphor is that the church is the bride of Christ (Eph 5:22-32). Again, the Bible disrupts our modern sensibilities and practices on the topic.

Yes, a lifelong covenant between two people is one of the most beautiful witnesses to both God's love and the human capacity to love. The healthiest marriages I know are *holy* indeed. They are holy because a *holy God* is in the center of them in a kind of divine love triangle. They are holy because two people have decided to love each other unconditionally, and they rechoose that commitment every day. They are holy because love is holy, not because a church pronounced the union "official."

I agree with Amie Martin's assessment in the last chapter of this book that "the current theology of marriage is not just *not* supported by scripture, tradition, reason, and experience, it's actually wounded hundreds of thousands of people. It is one of the great harms we [the church] have done to the world." The newly arising church of the 21$^{st}$ century needs to seek the healing of these wounds.

Has the church sacrificed "love for God and neighbor" on the idolatrous bed of romance? Have we placed a faulty ideology of "soul mates" who make each other complete, above a theology of union with Christ? When the church becomes the handmaiden of the state, the results are often devastatingly bad.

This book should come with a warning label, because once you see the truth you won't be able to unsee it. Read on if you dare. Amie Martin will show us why the church should go out of the marriage business.

-Michael Adam Beck, pastor, professor, author, Director of Fresh Expressions for The United Methodist Church, Director of Fresh Expressions House of Studies at United Theological Seminary.

# PREFACE

This is the first volume in a proposed series called the *Going out of Business Series*. This series is really an analysis of modern ecclesiology. It provides deep theological reflection on the nature, structure, and witness of the modern western church. What is the church's business? Where has the church perhaps overextended her power and reach? And what are the practical repercussions for her life and witness now?

The first era of church history, The Early Church Era, lasted approximately 300-400 years after Jesus lived on earth. It was a time of rapid, organic growth. The disciples mostly gathered around tables in homes in urban areas. They ate together. They told stories about Jesus. They learned how to live and love like him in their community and taught one another how to do so. They became known for socioeconomic and ethnic diversity, generosity, piety, and care for the sick, the poor, the orphan and widow. In many places they faced discrimination and persecution by more powerful pagan or Jewish groups. As they sent people with good news of Jesus throughout the Greco-Roman world, more pockets of these grassroots, local churches sprang up. Most gatherings did not have large, impressive buildings in which to gather yet. Leaders had to mobilize quickly and multiply into new locations. The rapid growth was astounding, from just a few hundred Jesus followers to an estimated 25 or 35 million by the fourth century! An unparalleled movement in human history. There were many different expressions of church and varied beliefs and practices.

The next era is often referred to as Christendom. During Christendom, the church enjoyed wealth, political power, and societal influence. What used to be a small minority had blossomed into a dominant majority. The hierarchy of the church solidified. The Roman Empire of the west became the "Holy Roman Empire." Popes and emperors ruled the people hand-in-hand. During this time, the church in the east was also central to the Byzantine Empire.

Understandably, when Christianity became a majority religion, things changed. Many of the simple ways of the early church were forgotten or replaced during Christendom. From the Middle Ages to the Reformation and even lingering into the modern church, many church buildings have been large and ornate. Many church rules have become legalistic and cumbersome. Many new practices developed beyond simple discipleship, worship, spiritual formation of the common people. Some of the new ways of doing things have been beautiful, impressive, or deeply meaningful for so many people, but others were harmful.

There are many areas of society in which the church began to do business that are superfluous. A few largely unexamined practices from Christendom that linger today and are arguably not essential to the mission of the church. Hasn't the church always been in the wedding business? The entertainment business? The law-making business? Has the ordination business always been as cumbersome as it is now? If the answers are "no," perhaps it is time to re-evaluate the church's role in each of these businesses from a biblical, historical, logical, and experiential lens. I hope this series will help the struggling church once again find her faithful place in a western society in which Christianity is losing power and influence. What is essential to her mission and witness? Perhaps there are certain areas the church needs to let go of in order to prioritize her resources and focus on her first love. Maybe she would be healthier and more faithful if she considered which areas are necessary for *Going out of Business.*

I would also like to express my gratitude for all of those who helped make this volume possible. Several scholars and thinkers took their time reading previous drafts and offering helpful feedback and conversation, including Troy Martin, Henry H. Knight III, Mike Gillen, Erika Gravely, Angie Colina McNeil, Cassie O'Brien Graham, Casey Sigmon, Michael Beck, Jon Davis, Cindy Evans, Whitney Fossum, and Jeren Rowell. I am especially grateful to Michael Beck for writing the foreword to this volume. Special thanks must also be given to Audra Spiven and Sheryl Martin for their careful review of the work during the editing process and for preparing it for print, to Higher Life Publishing for their collaboration on the series, and to Aspen D. Alva for cover design.

Amie Martin

# INTRODUCTION

I initially wrote this book as a personal research project in order to better understand and decide my own pastoral approach to officiating weddings. I felt called by God to be a pastor, teacher, preacher, truth-teller, servant, spiritual caregiver, disciple-maker, fighter for justice, and lover of God and people. But if I were honest, the role of wedding officiant and agent of the state felt uncomfortable. I wasn't sure that God had called me to such a role. It felt like more of a cultural expectation than a spiritual one, but I wasn't sure why I felt that way until I started researching.

Additionally, storms were raging around me about for whom clergy people were allowed to perform weddings in the church. Traditionalists insist homosexuality is incompatible with Christian teaching based on their interpretation of Scripture, and progressives decry painful and discriminatory practices. While I could respect the convictions of people who hold both positions, every conversation I have witnessed has left me frustrated. It felt like something important was missing—but what was it?

Not only this, but the first church I served after I graduated from seminary went through a deeply painful and wounding season of disaffiliation from the denomination which gave her birth. As the associate pastor, I experienced so much misinformation, politicking, and agenda-driven secret legal action that I questioned whether I wanted to be in ministry anymore at all. Even though the leadership still resists admitting it publicly, this disaffiliation was driven mainly by fear of the looming changes in the denomination around the wedding practice and full inclusion of LGBTQIA+ persons.

So, I began sifting through research about the role of the clergyperson and the worship building in Scripture and two millennia of Christian history. As I did, the picture became clearer. As I also added reflection on my own experience of God's grace within the church, coupled with my cultural upbringing about romance, I felt like I had truly gained an appropriate, although unconventional, pastoral approach to wedding ministry. Even though my conclusions are different from most church leadership practices, my hope is that you give this work serious consideration.

# Introduction

I am an ordained clergy member in the North American United Methodist tradition, however, the insights from the research in this book can be useful to any student of culture or history, or anyone who is interested in religious practice as it relates to nuptials, laypersons, clergy, or clergy-in-training, and persons in any strand of Christian tradition, or even critics of religion. It will help each of us think in new, different, and more informed ways about the current practice of church control over wedding ceremonies, and what alternative models that have worked in the past and that might pave a way for our future.

# Chapter 1

## The Missing Question in the Church's Debate on Human Sexuality

I will share with you a gross and obvious understatement: Debates involving human sexuality have swiftly and catastrophically divided the Western church in the past several decades.

These debates and church splits have been particularly prominent in mainline Protestant churches. Not surprisingly, mainline Protestants have also experienced the greatest decline in membership numbers. According to Pew Research, "Mainline Protestants have declined at a faster rate than any other major Christian group, including Catholics and evangelical Protestants."[1] The Episcopal Church, which reached its peak attendance in the 1960s, has accelerated its decline over the last 25 years during its lengthy process to divide over

---

[1] Michael Lipka, "Mainline Protestants Make Up Shrinking Number of U.S. Adults," Pew Research Center, May 18, 2015, https://www.pewresearch.org/fact-tank/2015/05/18/mainline-protestants-make-up-shrinking-number-of-u-s-adults/.

human sexuality. After the release of the 2019 data, the *Episcopal News Service* published Rev. Dwight Zscheile's forecast: "The overall picture is dire—not one of decline as much as demise within the next generation unless trends change significantly. . . . At this rate, there will be no one in worship by around 2050 in the entire denomination."[2] Similarly, the largest Presbyterian denomination, PCUSA, whose peak membership in 1965 was 4.25 million members, has been debating human sexuality for more than three decades.[3] During this time, the membership has been in strong and steady decline. In 2019, the PCUSA reported roughly 1.3 million members left, losing roughly 35 percent of its members in the preceding decade.[4]

---

[2] Egan Millard, "2019 Parochial Reports Show Continued Decline and a 'Dire' Future for the Episcopal Church," *Episcopal News Service*, October 16, 2020, https://www.episcopalnewsservice.org/2020/10/16/2019-parochial-reports-show-continued-decline-and-a-dire-future-for-the-episcopal-church/.

[3] Leslie Scanlon, "PC(USA) Releases 2020 Statistical Report," *The Presbyterian Outlook*, April 22, 2021, https://pres-outlook.org/2021/04/pcusa-releases-2020-statistical-report/. The 4.25 million represents the total number of adherents of the two denominations at the time who would eventually merge to form what is now the PCUSA.

[4] Presbyterian Church USA, "Summaries of Statistics, Comparative Summaries," Presbyterian Church (USA), https://www.pcusa.org/site_media/media/uploads/oga/pdf/compsumstats2010.pdf and https://www.pcusa.org/site_media/media/uploads/oga/pdf/2019_stats_general.pdf.

# The Missing Question

The United Methodist Church, where I have been in full-time appointed ministry since 2018 and ordained as an elder since 2021, is particularly exposed right now, and also on the brink of potential collapse.[5] The General Conference of 2020, which was to prove decisive in offering a protocol for amicable separation over human sexuality, has been postponed for three consecutive years. A new splinter denomination called the Global Methodist Church was declared May 1, 2022. Amid denominational chaos and the desire to avoid the disastrous trends set by other mainline denominations that have gone before us, I am deeply worried about our current hyper-focus on human sexuality. As a United Methodist clergyperson, I was trained to approach difficult moral questions and dilemmas

---

[5] The status of the UMC as of 2022: The General Conference of the United Methodist Church, a worldwide denomination, has met every four years since 1968, when the denomination was formed. After the General Conference of 2016, the issues relating to human sexuality were not satisfactorily resolved. The leaders of the denomination did not feel they could wait another four years before discussing an adequate way forward, so in a historic break from tradition, a Special General Conference was called that met in February 2019 in St. Louis, Missouri. Millions of dollars later, after much expectation, strife, and media coverage, that assemblage also failed to produce a solution. The regularly scheduled 2020 General Conference was postponed until 2021 due to COVID, then postponed again until 2022. In 2022, it was postponed until 2024, again because of COVID. Meanwhile, the splintering of United Methodists in the United States continues to snowball.

primarily by using the Outlerian Quadrilateral (commonly referred to as the Wesleyan Quadrilateral). It is a four-part approach to decision-making for theology and practice, taking into consideration these four elements:

- Scripture (both the Hebrew Bible and New Testament)

- Tradition (how the Christian church across cultures and past centuries has lived out its witness)

- Reason (the application of cogent reasoning, plausible argument, and logical thought)

- Experience (interpreting grace through the lens of an individual's own life events)

I have witnessed firsthand many debates involving human sexuality within the church. While there are quite a few areas of contentious disagreement, what I have noticed is that the following claims seem to be ubiquitously agreed:

    1. All persons are of sacred worth and loved by God.[6]

---

[6] Wesleyan Covenant Association, "About the WCA," Wesleyan Covenant Association, https://wesleyancovenant.org/about-page/#1533314242168-c269fe11-86cb. Although traditionalists are sometimes heavily caricatured as denying the sacred worth of persons in the LGBTQIA+ community, these sorts of generalized stereotypes can be harmful. The WCA articulates their official stance on human dignity here, affirming that "every person must be afforded compassion, love, kindness, respect, and dignity."

2. Marriage and human sexuality are somehow deeply theologically significant.[7]

3. A clergyperson is the sanctioned representative of the church to perform the legal solemnization of weddings.[8]

4. Part of the business of a church must include solemnization of weddings.

For a long time, I uncritically accepted all these claims. After all, these four claims weren't the items that seemed to be up for debate. Instead, debate revolved around which type of marriage was compatible with Christian practice. All members of the clergy in my circles, regardless of where they fall on the theological spectrum, seemed to agree upon the above claims. Why stir up any more trouble than we already have?

---

[7] There is a broad spectrum of belief about how marriage and human sexuality "should" be handled by faithful Christians, but all seem to agree that it is an important part of life and that God cares about and wants to be honored by and involved in our intimate relationships.

[8] *The Book of Discipline of the United Methodist Church: 2016* (Nashville: United Methodist Publishing House, 2016), ¶ 340, "Responsibilities and Duties of Elders and Licensed Pastors,": "(3) To perform the ecclesial acts of marriage and burial. (a) To perform the marriage ceremony after due counsel with the parties involved and in accordance with the laws of the state and the rules of the United Methodist Church. The decision to perform the ceremony shall be the right and responsibility of the pastor."

But, since sincere Christian clergy and laypeople whom I love were still at an impasse regarding human sexuality, I wondered if it could be possible that we were all operating from a faulty foundation. I decided to review each of the above claims through the lens of the Outlerian Quadrilateral. I didn't have to spend much time before I came to the conclusion that the first and second claims had harmonious support in all four areas of Scripture, tradition, reason, experience. The biblical witness across the entire canon strongly teaches that all persons—regardless of race, ethnicity, gender, class, ability, age, or sexuality—are created in the image of God and are valued and deeply loved by God. So also tradition, reason, and experience sing in thousands of different voices a unified chorus about the intrinsic, sacred worth of all of humanity. This message of self-worth and personal value is an ongoing affirmation that every person alive needs to hear.

As far as the second claim about the significance of marriage, there also exists an overwhelming number of stories, warnings, poems, metaphors, and commandments about marriage and human sexuality within Christian Scripture and tradition. These things seem to matter to God, and reason and experience can help us understand why. The God revealed in

Jewish and Christian Scripture is interested and involved in earthly activity and human history. Marriage and sexuality within the individual and corporate Christian life have a powerful impact on individuals, families, and communities. Sometimes the impact is life-giving, sometimes destructive, but it is impactful and important, nonetheless.

It was the third and fourth claims on the list that I began to question. Had anyone run these claims through the gamut of the Outlerian Quadrilateral?[9] What *scriptures* address or support these claims involving the specific role of clergypersons and churches in weddings? How far back does Christian *tradition* insist that an ordained clergyperson sanction and solemnize weddings? What logical arguments can be made to support or oppose these claims (*reason*)? Where has the church's mandatory involvement in the wedding business gotten us (*experience*)?

I have witnessed many hostile, antagonistic, combative arguments between clergy or laypersons on both sides of this issue. But even for all the thoughtful, caring, open-minded discussions about church and sexuality, the greatest litmus test

---

[9] This is the missing question in the church's debate on human sexuality.

that ultimately divides clergy is this question: *Will you officiate a same-sex wedding ceremony?*

To which conscience-stricken traditionalist clergy must ultimately respond, "No, I could not in good faith do so."

Similarly, there is the question: *Will you continue to discriminate against LGBTQIA+ persons with regard to wedding ceremonies and deny them equal inclusion and rights within the ecclesial life of the church?*

To which the conscience-stricken progressive clergy must ultimately respond, "No, I could not in good faith do so."

Friends, colleagues, faithful pastors, bishops, shared sacred orders—we remain at an impasse. This book is, therefore, a Quadrilateral quest. I determined to research Scripture and tradition and consider reason and experience to evaluate the origins, history, and future implications of our current wedding practices. What must we keep, and what must we let go? What should the role of church and clergy be in wedding ceremonies?

Only God is holy, holy, holy. But just how holy is matrimony?

# Chapter 2

## Scripture: The Presence of Clergy in Bible Weddings

Many people, even the nonreligious and those who do not actively practice Christianity, want a "church wedding." Many cannot imagine a wedding that does not involve a priest, pastor, or minister officiating. Perhaps the motivation for some couples is to feel like they have God's blessing on their marriage. Perhaps some want to present a public indication of their desire to include God in their relationship. Or perhaps they are simply carrying out a perfunctory cultural expectation with very little religious motivation or meaning. Whatever the reason for desiring a clergy-led church wedding, every clergyperson I've ever met seems to assume that the role of wedding officiant is part and parcel of ordained pastoral duties. In my experience within the American Protestant tradition, the clergy role usually includes guiding the whole experience: rehearsal, opening the ceremony, recitation of liturgies, telling jokes, giving biblical marriage advice and/or sharing a homily, leading the couple in their vows, inviting them to exchange rings, officially joining them in holy matrimony, and signing the certificate that must be filed with the state. When clergy function in a priestly role, they are in a posture of representing God. In both the Roman Catholic and Eastern Orthodox traditions, marriage is even counted as one of the sacraments of the church.

Some people may assume that the Bible is the reason behind the church doing things this way. So, what does Scripture say about the role of a clergyperson and the church building in wedding rites? I can answer this question with one word: nothing. There is no scriptural example at all for a clergyperson to preside, officiate, sanction, give permission, or represent God in wedding ceremonies. This gaping absence includes both the Hebrew Bible (Old Testament) and the New Testament. As a matter of fact, for all the thousands of pages of holy writ, there is only one instance in all of Scripture that even mentions the *presence* of a clergyperson at a wedding, but he is clearly a guest (John 2:1-12).

There are dozens of marriages described in the Hebrew Bible. The first is the unnamed couple in Genesis 1. This first example is not a formal marriage rite *per se*; instead, it more so describes the divine act of creation: "So God created humans in his image, in the image of God he created them; male and female he created them. God blessed them, and God said to them, 'Be fruitful and multiply. . .'" (vv. 27–28a). In this first creation account, the living God created this first archetypal couple, blessed them, and instructed them to reproduce. As the story unfolds, God continues to be present and active in their relationship. No other priestly mediator was available.

In the second creation account in Genesis 2, the first couple is also interestingly unnamed. At first there is a genderless human prototype called *adam* (אָדָם), which in Hebrew is literally a play on words that mean either "red" (אָדֹם) or "ground" (אֲדָמָה). This word simply indicates a being that God formed from the ground. By itself, the Hebrew word *adam* tells us nothing about the sex or gender of the created being. Only after the "partner" (vv. 18, 20) is formed are the distinctive Hebrew words for "man" (*ish/ysh*, אִישׁ) and "woman" (*ishah*, אִשָּׁה) used for the first time (vv. 23, 24). God thus made genders—a man and a woman—out of this formerly genderless human prototype, the *adam*. The partner is not given the name "Eve" until Genesis 3:20, after the fall of humanity. She receives a name that connects her to her reproductive capabilities.

In this second marriage-like account in Genesis 2, again the living God is involved in the act of creation and places the couple together. Jesus later reminds the people that God Godself is actually the priest of the marriage covenant (Matthew 19:6). Sometimes clergy point to this biblical principle of God's role in the marriage covenant to defend their own priestly functions. They may explain that they are the stand-in representatives for God in the marriage covenant. But, even though God's priestly function in the marriage covenant can be seen in Scripture, the human clergy role is not. The function of human Jewish priests and Christian leaders in the New Testament is almost entirely for worship, spiritual formation of the community, and prophetic witness, and it did not involve any wedding responsibilities.

Many more people are clearly coupled throughout the rest of Genesis, but we aren't given details about how the couplings happen: Cain/wife, Lamech (who had two wives and represents the first of many instances of polygamy), Noah/wife, Noah's sons/wives, Abram/Sarai, Nahor/Milcah, Lot/wife, Lot's daughters/husbands, Judah/Shua, Er/Onan/Tamar, Esau/wives, Joseph/Asenath, and many more.

The first marriage coupling that is described in detail can be found in Genesis 24. An elderly Abraham charges his trusted servant to go back to his country of origin and find a wife for his son Isaac. God chooses Rebekah for Isaac and reveals this choice to Abraham's servant while they are at the well drawing water. Rebekah's father Bethuel and brother Laban give permission for her to go back with Abraham's servant and become Isaac's wife. Rebekah also chooses to go. After Rebekah and Isaac meet, Isaac takes her into his deceased mother's tent, and "she became his wife" (v. 67). Thus, the marriage rite is a family affair. Fathers negotiate, perhaps consult other members of the family, and an agreement between families is reached. There is no human priest or religious minister officiating, sanctioning, representing God, or giving permission. Similarly, in Jacob's marriages to Leah and Rachel, the arrangements are made within the family. Laban, the bride's father, makes a deal with Jacob, the groom. Another detail of ancient marriage ceremony and practice emerges in this narrative. Laban (father of the bride) gathers the community together and hosts a feast (29:22).

The practice of a community wedding feast reappears in Judges 14:12, where it is more specifically described as a

17

customary seven-day wedding feast. The marriage feast also appears in the later parables, stories, and sayings of Jesus: Matthew 22:1–14; 25:1–13; Luke 12:35–38; 14:7–11; and John 2:1–12. Nowhere in any of these biblical stories is there any instance of an officiant of the church or synagogue publicly solemnizing any wedding ceremony. Apart from the rabbi Jesus, who attends the wedding feast at Cana in John 2, the presence of a religious authority is excluded in every other biblical wedding account. Even in John 2, Jesus is depicted as a guest at the wedding banquet, not as someone who has been asked to occupy an official, clergy-related role. Some may argue that, according to John 2, the role of a religious official at a wedding is to bless the couple because Jesus multiplied the wine—yet Jesus was reluctant to perform this miracle and seems to have only done so at the insistent request of his mother.

In Tobit 7–8 we see perhaps the most descriptive marriage ceremony in all of Scripture.[10] Tobias asks Raguel (the bride's father) for Sarah's hand in marriage. Raguel then formally offers a blessing to the couple, in essence supplying

---

[10] Tobit is a book within the Protestant Apocrypha and considered deuterocanical and part of the Biblical canon of the Roman Catholic, Christian Orthodox, and Jewish traditions.

the role of officiant: "She is given to you from today and forever. May the Lord of heaven, my son, guide and prosper you both this night, and grant you mercy and peace" (Tob. 7:11). Again, Raguel takes his daughter Sarah by the hand and gives him to Tobias, saying, "Take her to be your wife in accordance with the law and decree written in the book of Moses. Take her and bring her safely to your father. And may the God of heaven let your journey go smoothly and in his peace" (v. 12). Raguel then writes a marriage contract and begins the customary feast. For modern readers, there is a noticeable absence of any clergyperson to conduct any part of a wedding ceremony, nor is any sort of sacred building, temple, or synagogue involved.

Official wedding business in the Bible is overwhelmingly a family and community affair. It was the family—namely fathers and grooms—who negotiated marital agreements. In biblical cultures and contexts, the patriarch of the family sometimes consulted the women and brides in these decisions, but permission or sanction was never needed, requested, or given by any priest or other representative of God. This power resided solely among families and the wedding couples. The family also invites the larger community of neighbors, friends, and clansmen to celebrate with a wedding feast.

One may rightly argue that before the Mosaic covenant, there were no clergypersons or priests available to perform matrimonial duties. Although there were no Jewish clergy before the Mosaic covenant, there are still no mentions of weddings or marital rituals described in the lengthy descriptions of the priestly role even after the cultic Levitical priesthood is instituted. Instead, priests and clergypersons perform many other duties for the religious community in the Bible. They oversee proper worship, teach, interpret Scripture, baptize, and share prayers and prophecies. But we have no biblical evidence that they ever solemnized *one single wedding.*

To be clear, I am not operating from a hermeneutic that anything not explicitly found in Scripture should not be practiced. Nor does my hermeneutic suggest that anything not explicitly forbidden in Scripture is permitted. Instead, I want to evaluate our modern wedding practice through all four sources of authority in the Outlerian Quadrilateral to invite the church to reconsider the usefulness of the practice for the ongoing mission of God in the world.

## Scripture: The Presence of Clergy

Among the four elements of the Quadrilateral, Scripture is considered primary as a resource for belief and practice. So, why do both traditionalists and progressives within the modern Christian church seem to *insist* that 1) a clergyperson should be the sanctioning representative of the church to perform the legal solemnization of weddings, and 2) that part of the business of a church must include solemnization of weddings? These practices cannot be found in Scripture. What grounds are there for the insistence of this practice? We must investigate the next part of the Quadrilateral to answer that question, looking into the history and tradition of the church.

# Chapter 3

## Tradition: The Historical Role of Clergy in Weddings

We do not have much information about how early Christians married. In fact, the absence of marriage theology and wedding practice in ante-Nicaean literature is remarkable, especially compared to later periods of Christian history. The very absence of discussion on this topic may indicate how decentralized marriage and wedding practices were in the mission of the early church. From what we can piece together, however, it was different from current Christian wedding practices. According to James Ponzetti and Barbara Horkoff Mutch, "During the advent of Christianity and for several centuries thereafter, marriage was typically an informal, private affair. . . . Matrimony was simply a secular association of a man and a woman."[11] I want to emphasize the words used to describe marriage in early Christianity: *informal*, *private*, *secular*.

---

[11] James J. Ponzetti and Barbara Horkoff Mutch, "Marriage as Covenant: Tradition as a Guide to Marriage Education in the Pastoral Context," *Pastoral Psychology* 54, no. 3 (2006): 216.

Consistent with Scripture, the witness of early Christian tradition does not seem to include clergy-officiated weddings in sacred buildings. One may argue there were few, if any, sacred buildings in which to hold ceremonies during this early stage of Christian development. Even so, the church was able to survive and thrive during this period and nonetheless maintain a focused and effective time of growth for the kingdom of heaven in the absence of this practice. Even without access to public sacred buildings, there were still active members of the clergy during this age, including deacons, elders, and bishops.

Because Christianity began as a movement within Judaism, we can probably assume that marriage rites and ceremonies in early Christianity resembled those within Judaism. In the Talmudic period, during the third century CE and beyond, we have descriptions of what has been an ongoing practice of two stages within the official marriage rite: first betrothal and then marriage. Scholars do believe these descriptions reflect an earlier practice, probably also including New Testament times. According to the Talmud, betrothal could be achieved in one of three ways. The most common was a written contract, as seen in the story of Tobit. However, it could also be achieved through the payment of money or even cohabitation, which was permitted but came with more social stigma. Betrothals were binding. It was considered a divorce to break off a betrothal (see Matthew 1:19). Betrothal often lasted a year or more and traditionally concluded when the young woman reached puberty and her father brought her bloody garment or bed linens to the groom to prove she was ready to consummate the marriage.

On the wedding day, the couple fasted and confessed sins. They wore crowns, and the bride processed with her veil and her entourage down the streets from her house to the groom's house. There the gathered community enjoyed a feast, music, dancing. The family wrote a contract, and the groom himself typically pronounced a specific set of seven blessings at the feast.[12] There is still no mention of official clergy involvement. Similar to accounts in the Bible, the weddings took place in the towns, streets, and homes of the community. They did not take place in the temples, synagogues, or other sacred spaces. According to rabbinic sources, it wasn't until the post-Talmudic period (seventh century CE) that a rabbi took

---

[12] Ponzetti and Mutch, "Marriage as Covenant," 216.

over the saying of the blessings.[13] Long before that time, Christianity had already evolved into a distinct movement.

Within early Christian tradition, there is a mention of the clergy role in marriage in a letter from Ignatius to Polycarp, allegedly written in the early second century. In it, Ignatius says: "But it becomes both men and women who marry, to form their union with the approval of the bishop, that their marriage may be according to God, and not after their own lust. Let all things be done to the honour of God."[14] The very fact that Ignatius deemed it necessary to make an argument for the bishop permitting Christian marriage means it was not the common practice. Ignatius also had uncommonly strong views of the weight of the episcopacy, claiming "nothing in the congregation should happen without the bishop."[15] His sentiments may not have been widely shared. Even so, Korbinian Ritzer claims that Ignatius does not mean the bishop should have a role in conducting the wedding ceremony, but that earnest Christians should seek his consent. Ritzer also

---

[13] Kenneth Stevenson, *Nuptial Blessing: A Study of Christian Marriage Rites* (New York: Oxford University Press, 1983), 8.

[14] Ignatius, "Epistle of Ignatius to Polycarp," 5 (ANF 1:95).

[15] Ignatius, "Epistle of Ignatius to the Smyrnaeans," 8 (1:89).

contends that "There is no evidence of the existence of this kind of custom [of obtaining permission from the bishop] that can be found in the first three hundred years. The opposite proves itself...In any case, this practice was not enforced."[16] Marriages were also still celebrated at home and within the community during this time.

In addition, the early church existed within the context of the Roman Empire. The Roman view of marriage had a strong influence on Christianity during its early development— in particular, the idea that a man was the head of the household and had decision-making power as *pater familias* over all the activities, lives, and arrangements (marital or otherwise) of those who lived within the household. Thus, the male heads of households typically decided their children's or slaves' marriages. "In short, [Roman] marriages were merely financial and sexual arrangements aimed at strengthening the community.

---

[16] Korbinian Ritzer, *Formen, Riten, und Religiöses Brauchtum der Eheschliessung in den Christlichen Kirchen des Ersten Jahrtausends* (Münster: Aschendorff, 1962), 29–31. This is my translation of the German original, as Ritzer is commenting on Ignatius's letter to Polycarp: "Es ist für das Vorhandensein eines derartigen Brauches in den ersten drei Jahrhunder -ten kein Beleg zu finden. Das Gegenteil lässt sich beweisen...Durchgesetzt hat sie sich jedenfalls nicht."

Love had no part in such arrangements."[17] This claim from Ponzetti and Mutch may be a bit of an overstatement since there are some Hellenistic romance novels that indicate some marriages were deeply romantic. But it still reflects the strong influence of the social and financial realities of the day.

The Roman requirement for marriage was consent by simple private agreement. In the absence of required involvement of church and clergy, most Christians followed the law of the land and had civil weddings recognized by the state. The difference between a legal marriage and a concubinage in Roman law was that a socially acceptable legal marriage necessitated the man marry a woman of his own social class. The Roman wife was to share the legal rights and privileges afforded by the social status of her husband. "The quality of rank between the parties was, in the aristocratic society of Romans, the peculiar characteristic of marriage. Through this essential element it was made distinct from a mere cohabitation."[18] It was uncommon for two people to marry who belonged to different social classes in the Roman Empire, but

---

[17] Ponzetti and Mutch, "Marriage as Covenant," 218.

[18] Emile Stocquart, *Marriage in Roman Law* (New Haven, CT: Yale Law Journal Company, 1907), 303–327.

when they did, the bride adopted the social status of the groom. This civil arrangement was problematic for many Christians, who blurred the lines of social class within their gatherings. According to historian Justo Gonzalez, secret church marriages may have begun as an alternative solution to legal marriages in order to preserve the social status of a Christian woman who may have been marrying beneath her class.[19] Still, clergy involvement in this type of wedding was the exception and not the rule and was based on providing a functional alternative option for those who needed or wanted to preserve social privilege. It was *not* because of a widely developed theology about marital sacredness.

There is an observable lack of discussion of Christian wedding practice or marriage theology in the first three centuries of Christian tradition. Weddings were mainly private affairs outside the official jurisdiction of the church. Whereas marriage in the Jewish tradition was expected and normative, Christianity innovated through the promotion of celibacy and singleness. Sadly, this innovation largely seems to have been lost. Ponzetti and Mutch claim that it wasn't until Christianity became the official religion of the state in the fourth century

---

[19] Justo L. Gonzalez, *The Story of Christianity: The Early Church to the Dawn of the Reformation* (New York: HarperOne, 2010), 115.

that church leaders "began to insist that the church had her own marriage law predicated on divine law. This distinction served to set Christian marriage apart from the civil arrangements that had sufficed during the first three centuries of the church's existence."[20]

Even so, no consistent rules governed marriage within the church, even up to the reforms of the late eleventh century. There was still widespread debate about what constituted a legitimate marriage. Most still believed mutual consent was enough, while some argued for evidence of sexual consummation or the necessity of the presence of a witness or member of the clergy.[21] In a writing from the seventh century, Bishop Isidore of Seville penned an argument for wedding nuptials to be blessed by a priest and in a church. Wedding ceremonies began moving from offsite homes to the steps of churches or cathedrals. Again, this bishop's effort to present a convincing rationale indicates the church did not yet have an authoritative, consistent practice and that there may have been an ongoing discussion about proper wedding rites. In addition, the deficit of literature on the subject may have been an

---

[20] Ponzetti and Mutch, "Marriage as Covenant," 220.

[21] Ponzetti and Mutch, "Marriage as Covenant," 221.

indication that this issue was not important to many church leaders of the time. In short, it is likely that many Christian weddings were still being held away from church buildings and without the blessing of a member of the clergy.[22]

During the twelfth century, the influence of courtly love changed attitudes toward romance and sexuality. Instead of a family arrangement based on financial and sexual agreements, people increasingly valued passion and romance. Theologians also began to write more about the mystical spiritual value of sexuality. This change in thought influenced many church theologians to consider marriage as a sacrament. Before the middle of the thirteenth century and for the first time in Christian tradition, three councils officially recognized marriage as a sacrament: Second Lateran Council in 1139, the Council of Verona in 1184, and the Fourth Lateran Council in 1215.[23]

When the Roman Catholic Church elevated marriage as an official sacrament of the church, priests were the only eligible officiants. This practice revealed the increasingly popular belief that God's grace was imparted during the ceremony. Thus, a sacramental wedding in a church was special

---

[22] Stevenson, *Nuptial Blessing*, 53.

[23] Ponzetti and Mutch, "Marriage as Covenant," 222.

in terms of God's grace, blessing, and involvement. Although the process was gradual and seemed to occur over several centuries, it was during this period of medieval Christian history that marriage officially moved into a central place in Christian theology and practice. The philosophy of Renaissance humanism and companionate marriage in the sixteenth century further emphasized personal intimacy and individual romantic choice within marriage.

I am not claiming that Christians during the first half of church history did not marry—many, if not most, did. Jesus was not anti-marriage, Paul was not anti-marriage, and Christianity was not anti-marriage (although Jesus, Paul, and Christian tradition may have expressed a preference toward singleness as the most useful state for holy living). Paul did also recommend the institution of marriage as a holy option available to Christians as they navigated their sexuality (see 1 Cor. 7). My exploration of tradition demonstrates that, consistent with the witness of Scripture, the first half of the Christian tradition did not *require* or *insist upon* a widespread practice of clergy involvement or the use of the sacred worship space for wedding rites, even though that has gradually become the norm for the second half of Christian tradition. Therefore, Christian tradition includes a long and effective era of decentralization of sex and marriage in both corporate religious practice and theology. It is thus conceivable to live out a faithful church witness without the norm or necessity of clergy-officiated church weddings.

Since both Scripture and tradition seem to give permission to exclude weddings from official church business, how does the church decide what is in the best interest of its people today? Reason and logical thought must become a necessary part of the discussion.

# Chapter 4

# Reason: Applying Logic to the Practice of Clergy-Led Weddings

After a brief study of the voices of Scripture and tradition, we now try to uncover the voice of reason. Reason is the part of the Quadrilateral that utilizes rational thought and seeks to come to logical conclusions. This chapter outlines the argument, counterargument, and concessions and refutations.

## Argument

> *If the church decided to cease offering clergy-officiated weddings in church buildings or at least redact the requirement or expectation for clergy to officiate weddings in their church buildings, this decision would have support from both Scripture and tradition and would allow the church to fulfill its mission more effectively.*

There is no uniform way for Christians to marry. Christians in the apostolic age fared well and maintained orthodox theology without the practice of clergy-officiated weddings. Christians in the early Middle Ages sometimes involved clergy in wedding rites and sometimes did not.

Christians in the later Middle Ages and in the Reformation and post-Reformation eras have consistently held clergy-officiated, church weddings.

The task of the church in every age is to make decisions that most effectively serve the mission and kingdom of God in its own context. This evaluation of culture and appropriate methodology has become an academic discipline called "missiology." What was the missiology of the early church? The early church found itself in a minority position and faced occasional persecution by the majority. The early church did not enjoy the luxury of large buildings and significant cultural influence. Therefore, the evangelistic strategy of the early church had to be one of *cautious infiltration.* The Christians infiltrated homes, businesses, and marketplaces with the counter-cultural witness of living with Jesus as Lord. From such a position, the essentials of the faith had to be central in practice and theology for the movement to survive. Therefore, the early church was less concerned with the practice of wedding nuptials. Since weddings were on the periphery of their religious practice, they continued the cultural tradition of celebrating wedding feasts in homes among friends and family.

# Reason: Applying Logic to the Practice

As the church of the Middle Ages found itself in an increasingly powerful position within society, the evangelistic strategy became one of *strategic assimilation*. To spread Christianity to pagan cultures, the church tried to Christianize formerly pagan holidays and traditions to try to assimilate pagan regions under Christian rule. In addition to adopting pagan wedding practices, such as the attire of veils and rings, the church Christianized the wedding ceremony by adding its own liturgy, clergy presence, and location. To bring this widely practiced cultural rite under the power of the church was intentional. Weddings became more of an opportunity for the church to exert further control over the daily lives of the people under its political power. It is important to note that strategic assimilation is most effective in a context where the church has significant political, social, and legal influence and power within the wider culture.

The question for the church in the United States now is: which strategy is most effective for the kingdom of God in our context? What missiology best fits? Is Christianity still a majority religion with loads of influence and power (like in the second half of Christian history), or has it become more of a minority movement (like in the early church)? How much influence, relevance, and political power does Christianity still hold in the U.S.?

After two decades of consistent and sharp decline for Christianity in the U.S., for the first time in U.S. history, those who claim to be members of a faith community are in the minority.[24] The imperialistic evangelistic strategy of Christendom that assimilated the culture may not be the strategy that is needed in this present time in the United States.

Furthermore, there has formed an alliance between church and state where weddings are concerned. The legal word for the role of a clergyperson in a wedding is "solemnization." In my home state of Missouri (and marriage solemnization laws vary by state), legal power is explicitly granted by the state to clergypersons and religious institutions:

> *Marriages may be solemnized by any clergyman, either active or retired, who is in good standing with any church or synagogue in this state. Marriages may also be solemnized, without compensation, by any judge, including a municipal judge. Marriages may also be solemnized by a religious society, religious institution, or religious organization of this state, according to the regulations and customs of the*

---

[24] Jeffrey M. Jones, "U.S. Church Membership Falls below Majority for First Time," Gallup, March 29, 2021, https://news.gallup.com /poll/341963/church-membership-falls-below-majority-first-time.aspx.

*society, institution or organization, when either*
*party to the marriage to be solemnized is a*
*member of such society, institution or*
*organization.*[25]

According to the law, the only persons with power in
my state to solemnize weddings are judges (an appropriate
agent of the state in my opinion) or a "clergyman" or religious
institution. Even as the terms in this passage reflect language
from several decades ago (there are also women clergy), this
whole statute remains peculiar. Why should ordination vows in
any denomination include performing a service for the state? In
the UMC *Book of Discipline*, conducting "the service of
marriage" is named directly after sacraments in the list of
"Responsibilities and Duties of Those Licensed for Pastoral
Ministry."[26] Along with the couple being married, clergy
members are usually the central figures throughout the
ceremony. At many Protestant wedding ceremonies, the person
officiating may conclude by saying, "By the power vested in
me, I now pronounce you husband and wife." What power is
this, and where does it come from? Is it divine power from God,

---

[25] Revised Statues of Missouri, XXX Stat. 451.100.1 (1998),
https://www.mo.gov/home-family/marriage-divorce/.

[26] *Book of Discipline of the United Methodist Church*, ¶316.

or is it granted by the State? If they suppose this power to be granted by God, what does that mean? Is a couple's union somehow more blessed if a member of the clergy joins them? Does God not recognize the union of the couple outside an official pronouncement of a clergyperson? Or, if this power is granted by the State, how appropriate is it for a clergyperson to summon the power of the State in the center of the holy space of Christian worship? It is especially surprising that in a country whose First Constitutional Amendment strives to separate the collusion of Church and State, the State seems willing to allow the church to overstep this stated boundary line with regard to legal coupling.

The state certainly doesn't compensate these ministers or churches for this time. In fact, notice that the legal statute is careful to point out that the judge is the one who will solemnize weddings "without compensation." The assumption here is that clergypersons or churches will collect compensation for solemnizing weddings (which they almost always do).

Here is the trade-off: the state gives the church and clergypersons the *power* to solemnize weddings, and in return for completing this state task, the church and clergypersons can *benefit financially.* One of the darkest sides of organized religion is exposed when it tangles its power with that of the state. This trend never ceases to amaze me within Christianity in particular, because Jesus so carefully avoided exploiting people or systems for financial gain or aligning himself with those in political power.

Another oddity of this particular statute about wedding solemnization is that it is the *only* instance of *active* legal power given to clergypersons or religious institutions. There are other instances where clergypersons are legally *exempted:* jury duty, military service, disclosure of confidential communications within pastoral counseling, and laws that prohibit unauthorized practice of psychology.[27] In each of these instances, the clergyperson is granted an exemption, so that they do *not* have to do something. The case of wedding solemnization is the only instance when the clergyperson is granted legal power to perform a state task and allowed to personally collect financial compensation for it.

It is also noteworthy that even in states whose solemnization statutes are more flexible, wedding solemnization remains part and parcel of an expected role of a clergyperson. Of course, when a minister officiates a wedding, there should be

---

[27] These include federal exemptions and exemptions that may vary by state.

much more than the legal task involved. The work of a minister is inherently spiritual and theological. But what exactly is this spiritual or theological good or service being offered by the Christian minister? Depending on which denomination or theological tradition, the answers may vary. Several answers may include: Permission to wed? Administration of a sacrament? Divine sanctioning or blessing of the union? An opportunity for testimony or evangelism? A perceived religious experience? An additional opportunity for worship? Premarital counsel (which is unfortunately not always part of the deal)? Event planning (does this one count as spiritual)? Most religious organizations offer these and other religious goods and services as part of the wedding business.

This conversation is much more sensitive particularly in Orthodox or Roman Catholic traditions in which Christian marriage is viewed as a sacrament and as such can only be administered by a professionally trained and licensed priest. And even though many protestant traditions do not define marriage as a sacrament, it is difficult to tell the difference in practice and treatment. The practice of clergy-officiated marriage in church buildings still seems to be held in high sentimental value, regardless of the Christian tradition to which one belongs. What spiritual or religious benefits would a couple actually forego if they chose not to utilize the services of a church or licensed minister in their wedding?

Perhaps clergy would do better to allow the state to conduct the legal business of the land while the church focuses instead on the mission-critical aspects of the clergy role that are necessary during times of minority influence.

What have been the mission-critical uses of clergy and sacred spaces consistently throughout history? The function of clergy and the use of sanctuaries in Judaism and early Christianity was mainly for worship, sacraments, and spiritual formation. The Jewish tabernacle and temple were used solely for sacrifice and worship. The place surrounding the ark of the covenant (the concentrated presence of God) was considered too sacred for any other activity. The fact that weddings were held in homes offsite was evidence of their lack of theological significance in comparison with the official, sacred-religious activity of the temple. Marriage, although significant in the lives of individuals and communities, was not the central business of the religion, which was instead the worship of God. Even today in Judaism, there is a theological hesitation to hold weddings inside a synagogue. Maurice Lamm, a leading rabbinical authority, stated, "*Halakhically*, it is preferred to hold the wedding service on the synagogue premises, but sensitivity should be shown in placing the *chuppah* in the inner sanctum of the synagogue. Historically, it was the presence of a symbolic bedchamber near the Ark. Despite this concern, weddings today are frequently held in the sanctuaries of orthodox synagogues."[28] Barbara Binder Kadden wrote, "Weddings may take place anywhere . . . sometimes held in the home of the groom or the bride. . . . They are also often held in the *synagogue grounds, or in a courtyard*."[29]

Within Christianity, weddings gradually moved from secular, community locations into the center of sacred spaces. When the church acquired public buildings during the Constantinian era, weddings were still mostly held offsite or in homes. At the Council of Carthage 398, priestly prayer was expected at the home location of the wedding. Over several centuries, the ceremony eventually moved to the steps of the

---

[28] Maurice Lamm, "The Location of a Jewish Wedding," Chabad-Lubavitch Media Center, n.d., https://www.chabad.org/library /article_cdo/aid/480509/jewish/The-Location-of-a-Jewish-Wedding.htm.

[29] Barbara Binder Kadden, "Jewish Weddings: When and Where They Happen," My Jewish Learning, n.d., https://www.myjewishlearning .com/article/time-place-for-a-jewish-wedding/, emphasis added, italics are mine.

cathedral, and finally—with the sacramentalization of marriage in the twelfth century—into the inner sanctuary of the church.

Not only the physical space, but also the role of a clergyperson has gradually moved from the periphery to the center in wedding ceremonies. What is the biblical role of a clergyperson in the lives of congregants who are marrying? Although the *biblical* role is not officiating or solemnizing, an argument can be made for providing counsel or blessing. Paul gave considerable marriage advice in his epistles, not because he was a clergy-for-hire offering a religious service but because he wanted to guide his flock toward holy living.

The importance of biblical premarital counsel cannot be emphasized enough. Many pastors I know do not require or even provide counsel before officiating the ceremonies for which they are paid extra. In favor of clergy-led premarital counseling, David Anderson argues, "The pastor or church should not simply be a servant of the state, meaning they will just perform any wedding. The pastor is a servant of Christ first."[30] Jennifer Barlow cites that Christians are more likely to divorce than non-Christians and claims that adequate marriage

---

[30] David Anderson, *Before God and These Witnesses: An Evangelistic Guide to Weddings*, PhD diss. (Liberty University, 2017), 15.

preparation of at least six to eight sessions, at least six months before the wedding ceremony, significantly decreases divorce rates.[31] Because most pastors are not adequately trained for or available to do this, Barlow recommends the use of a professional Christian counselor. Making plans for the wedding ceremony is not an adequate substitute for marriage preparation.

If a qualified clergyperson offers premarital preparation and support, it is arguably more of the difficult and less glamorous behind-the-scenes work. So other than financially, how does the church benefit from the more visible and powerful role in the wedding business? Instead of reaping many benefits, the church has made great sacrifices to preserve its stake in the marriage business. Marriage practice is swiftly becoming the sticking point that is splitting apart many mainline Protestant denominations. Idols reveal themselves not only by how we spend our time and money but also by what extent of destruction we allow. "In essentials, unity. In non-essentials, liberty, and in all things, charity."[32] Many arguments have been had over what is essential and non-essential in Christian faith

---

[31] Jennifer L. Barlow, "A New Model for Premarital Counseling within the Church," *Pastoral Psychology* 48, no. 1 (1999): 3.

[32] This quote is popularly attributed both to John Wesley and to St. Augustine of Hippo, but the original author remains unknown.

and practice. In our present situation there are two "essentials" that directly oppose each other: (1) the insistence on clergy-officiated, church-hosted weddings and (2) the insistence on the unity of the church. Which is more essential to the gospel?

Unity is a central theme of the gospel of Jesus Christ. Jesus prays specifically for the future movement of the Christian church in John 17, and his thesis is "that they may all be one. As you, Father, are in me and I am in you, may they also be in us . . ." (v. 21). The reason this is so important to Jesus is "so that the world may believe that you have sent me" (v. 21). He goes on to repeat both ideas to stress their importance. "The glory that you have given me I have given them, so that they may be one, as we are one, I in them and you in me, that they may become completely one, so that the world may know that you have sent me and have loved them even as you have loved me" (vv. 22–23).

So also the apostle Paul stresses how crucial unity is in the gospel message: "[Make] every effort to maintain the unity of the Spirit in the bond of peace" (Eph. 4:3). The specific work of the clergy is "to equip the saints for the work of ministry, for building up the body of Christ, until all of us come to the unity of the faith and of the knowledge of the Son of God, to maturity, to the measure of the full stature of Christ" (vv. 12–13). One of the main themes in Paul's first letter to the church in Corinth is one of unity: "Now I appeal to you, brothers and sisters, by the name of our Lord Jesus Christ, that all of you be in agreement and that there be no divisions among you, but that you be knit together in the same mind and the same purpose" (1 Cor. 1:10). Again Paul advises that there "be no dissension within the body" (12:25).

Unity is essential to the gospel. Clergy-officiated church weddings are not. Still, of all the valiant and exhaustive efforts that bishops, clergy, conferences, and jurisdictions have made to preserve the unity of the United Methodist Church over the past several years, none seems willing to give up the right and practice of church participation or control in the marriage business. An anti-gospel schism caused by nonessential theology or practice is allowed to remain in the church, even though that theology or practice has become an idol for which we are willing to sacrifice. We are not only sacrificing our focus on God's mission, but we are also sacrificing our collegial relationships, our prophetic witness in the world, and numerous souls who are so hurt by the discrimination or hypocrisy of the church that they wander away from God.

## Conclusion

Historically and scripturally, clergy-officiated weddings in a sanctuary need not be an essential practice of Christianity. The mission of the church may even be better served if clergy and sacred spaces returned to focus solely on worship and spiritual formation. The gradual movement of marriage from the periphery to a more central position throughout Christian history, both in location and clergy involvement, no longer serves the mission of the church. The gospel is more focused on the unity of the church, which is currently being sacrificed to preserve the central practice of clergy-officiated weddings held in sacred buildings. One way the church might both preserve its unity and its fidelity to worship of God alone would be to cease participation in the marriage business.

## Counterargument

*Clergy-officiated weddings held in sacred spaces benefit the church in many ways.*

**Tool for Evangelism**

Many churches have more unchurched people who attend wedding services throughout the year than regularly scheduled Sunday worship services. For many couples or their respective families, church weddings provide valuable opportunities to enter a church building and get to know a clergyperson. These opportunities are one of the best tools for evangelism that many churches have to influence the community and preach the gospel to those who would otherwise not hear it. If the church were to abandon this practice, it would lose one of its greatest evangelistic tools.

Further, coupling is part of human life. When the church has a significant role to play in coupling, the church can offer Christian influence in people's everyday lives and concerns. For the church to remain relevant in the wider society, it should not abandon the little ground and influence it has to participate in the community, including wedding ceremonies.

## Witness to Christian Marriage

Marriage is important to life, to faith, and to God. Marriage theology is discussed in many significant passages in the Bible, from the nature of created beings in Genesis 1 to the metaphor of the wedding of the Lamb to the church in Revelation 21. A Christian understanding of marriage that portrays a deep relationship of mutual love, care, submission, sacrifice, and support within a sacred covenant of faithfulness is a strong witness that the world desperately needs. Christian wedding ceremonies provide an opportunity to be a witness to such a theology of marriage. Couples can use a clergy-officiated church wedding as an opportunity to testify to their faith in God and their belief that God's grace will sustain their marriage.

## Concessions and Refutations

Yes, many unchurched people do enter church buildings for weddings and, as a result, experience Christian sermons, prayers, songs, and anecdotes. But how much true worship of Christ is central at weddings, as opposed to the worship of romance? Is this syncretistic portrayal of worship a faithful witness? Does the church win a point every time someone without religious affiliation merely enters the building? Is this benefit to the church enough to outweigh the cost of the practice of clergy-led church weddings? Do these unchurched guests participate in follow-up discipleship opportunities that bring them into regular participation in the community of faith? If weddings indeed are one of the greatest evangelism tools of a church, what does that say about the lack of embodied witness of the church as a community of forgiveness, grace, generosity, humility, peace, and justice? How effective are weddings as an evangelism tool for fulfilling the Great Commission of making disciples? How many baptisms result from wedding attendance?

Yes, God does care about marriage because God cares about every aspect of human life, with a special interest in

51

relationships, families, and how people treat one another. If clergy-officiated church weddings could provide a positive, biblical, consistent witness to the world of Christian marriage theology, then clergy-led church weddings would be a helpful practice. Instead, there is a blatant lack of unified witness to the meaning, practice, and theology of marriage within Protestantism in the U.S. that has hurt the overall witness and influence of the church in greater society. Not only is there deep and destructive conflict within Christianity, but Christians as a group are also statistically no more faithful to their marriage covenants than non-Christians. Perhaps the church's marred witness of marriage is not, in fact, the most effective testament the church has to communicate the love of God to the world.

# Chapter 5

## Experience: How God's Grace Helps Inform Our Practice

Experience is the resource within the Quadrilateral that makes this too distinctly Wesleyan. John Wesley realized that faith and real life go hand in hand. God the Holy Spirit is still active in the life of the church and its people. Beyond individual experience, the lived experience of people with a shared cultural context can provide valuable information to the spiritual effectiveness of certain religious beliefs or practices. For Wesley, the kind of experience that informs theological decision-making is specifically the experience of God's grace.

I graduated from high school in 1999. My adolescence was marked by the heavy-handed purity culture movement. An estimated 2.4 million teenagers signed a virginity pledge because of the *True Love Waits* movement.[33] Throughout my

---

[33] Lawrence K. Altman, "Study Finds That Teenage Virginity Pledges Are Rarely Kept," *New York Times* (March 10, 2004), https://www.nytimes.com/2004/03/10/us/study-finds-that-teenage-virginity-pledges-are-rarely-kept.html#:~:text=",-Continue%20reading%20the

upbringing, the purity culture ideals taught me that romantic heterosexual love and marriage were of paramount importance for a happy, successful, righteous Christian life. However, in my experience of God's grace, Jesus truly is the only One who has been my salvation and continued source of abundant life. Romantic love has been inconsistent for me.

In examining my cultural context, I begin to understand how my own views of marriage and romance have been shaped. Romance is a powerful idol in modern U.S.-American culture. Romantic themes dominate the entertainment industry, from music to movies to TV to social media and even advertising. The Beatles told the world that "love is all you need," while Tim McGraw testified that "your love saved me." Beyoncé claims that "your love can do what no one else can," and Justin Bieber sings about "running to the altar like a track star . . . because the way you hold me . . . feels so holy, holy, holy, holy, holy." Add to that the rom-com movie plots that are the same for hundreds of movies, changing only the settings and actors. The strong and consistent idolatrous message is that a person finds their ultimate satisfaction, salvation, or fulfillment in a deified romantic love in which they were destined either to find

&text=True%20Love%20Waits%20says%20that,Longitudinal%20Study%2
0of%20Adolescent%20Health.

or tragically lose. There are numerous examples, but just a few from my early years include: *The Princess Bride* (1987), *Pretty Woman* (1990), *Sleepless in Seattle* (1993), *The Notebook* (2004), *Love Is All You Need* (2012).

Not only do residents in the U.S. spend a significant amount of entertainment hours becoming intoxicated by the god of romance, but we also spend a significant amount of money on creating the perfectly ethereal wedding day. The wedding industry in the United States (pre-COVID) raked in more than $70 billion per year.[34] In this consumer-driven economy, entrepreneurs have not missed the opportunity to maximize profits by exploiting the deeply cherished idol of romantic coupling. From event planners to wedding websites and registries to flowers, decor, attire, and venues, to photography, hair and makeup, the average cost of a U.S.-American wedding in 2018 was $33,931.[35] This average includes Christians and non-Christians alike. Even the church has capitalized on fees for

---

[34] IBISWorld, "Wedding Services in the U.S.: Market Size 2005–2027," updated Dec 7, 2021, https://www.ibisworld.com/industry-statistics/market-size/wedding-services-united-states/.

[35] Liz Knueven, "The Average Wedding Cost $19,000 in 2020, about $10,000 Less Than the Year Before," *Business Insider*, June 3, 2021, https://www.businessinsider.com/personal-finance/how-much-does-a-wedding-cost. The average cost of weddings dropped significantly in 2020 because of COVID, but it is on the rise again.

space usage and offering ministers and musicians for hire (in many instances in the absence of adequate premarital counseling and preparation).

Idolatry is nothing new. Every culture has its own idols. But the church called to first-commandment faithfulness is to reject the idols of the culture around us and worship God alone. The Christian purity culture in which I was raised failed to do this. If anything, it only further deified the god of romance because heterosexual marriage was emphasized as one of the primary goals of life. I was taught that marriage would be especially divine, redemptive, and gratifying if both partners were virgins at the time of the wedding. Perhaps the idol has gradually infiltrated the church instead of the church infiltrating the wider culture. The gradual centralization of weddings in church theology and practice throughout the church's history is evidence of the infiltration of this idol.

Most of my social media connections are self-identified Christians and churchgoers, but a majority of wedding anniversary posts still demonstrate worship of the idol of romantic love. The following is an anonymous example of a post with a picture in 2021:

> Soon we will be celebrating 41 years in our
> marriage. This woman is my heart and soul. She

is my strength, my drive, my life. I love her without end.

Today is also her birthday. She is as lovely, as beautiful, as inspiring as the day we first met.

If my life could be summarized in a few words, it would be: "All because of you."

All my love always. Thank you for being my strength, my love, my everything. All my love, always, forever.

The idolatrous elements of this post are many. For another human being to be one's "heart and soul" competes with God, who desires our undivided hearts and souls. God wants to be our strength, our drive, our life, our "everything." Holiness strives to put God as central in our hearts, lives, and wills—not another human being. I hope my life could be summarized by the words, "All because of *Jesus*." The work of God is my salvation, not the romantic love of another human being.

One of the most telling indications that the idol of romantic love resides within Christianity is not only the prolific examples of similar social media posts written by Christians but also that these idolatrous public testimonies are accepted and largely unchallenged within Christian dialogue. Why aren't more clergy and laity speaking against such idolatry? In fact, many clergy people also participate in writing similar types of social media posts! This sort of idolatry has become so widely accepted among Christians that we do not even recognize it as idolatry. If I were viewing Christianity from the outside, I might be confused about who or what the true object of worship is. It is almost as if romantic coupling is a main tenet of the faith.

Another sign that the church has accepted the rampant cultural idol of romance is the cultural devaluation of singleness as a viable lifestyle even within the church. Although unpopular in our culture, singleness is an important biblical model of holiness. Jesus was single and truly human. Jesus even challenged his disciples to wrestle with consciously deciding whether to marry instead of automatically assuming a lifestyle of marriage (see Matthew 19:8–12). According to Jewish teaching, "So too, a single man is incomplete; his marriage is a completion and thus a transformation, acquiring for him a clean slate, spiritually."[36] Jesus was correcting a popular belief in Judaism by restoring singleness to an honorable state. Our current Protestant church culture has by and large reverted to the belief that Jesus spoke against—namely, that the state of marriage is superior to the state of singleness.

---

[36] Daniel Feldman, "The Development of Minhag as a Reflection on Halakhic Values: the Pre-wedding Fast," *Tradition* 35, no. 1 (2001): 44–54.

The apostle Paul gives a more detailed argument in his pastoral advice on marriage and singleness in 1 Corinthians 7. In this chapter, Paul seems to teach that singleness is a commendable station—but that doesn't mean marriage is not. Beth Phillips advises, "The point really is not whether one is single or married. God gives both stations in life as gifts; neither should be devalued or avoided. The point is that whatever our marital status, we must not let anxieties of this world cloud our undivided devotion to Christ."[37]

In contradiction to the biblical witness, my experience of the teaching of the church has not given singleness a voice at all. Of the hundreds of sermons, Bible studies, and workshops I have experienced in the church concerning marriage (and within Christian purity culture), I have never heard a sermon, Bible study, or workshop seriously investigate the lifestyle of singleness. Single people have also not been given equal status within the church. I was in a church board meeting that discriminated against hiring a gifted, Spirit-filled pastor solely on the basis of that pastor's single status. Those board members argued that this pastor "could not possibly understand married

---

[37] Beth Phillips, "1 Corinthians 7 and Singleness in the Church," *Leaven*, Vol. 9, Issue 3, Article 4 (2001), https://digitalcommons.pepperdine .edu/leaven/vol9/iss3/4.

people" and even that existing with no "outlet" for sexual urges might lead this pastor "into temptation." Would Jesus or Paul have been deemed insufficient ministers in this same church? The mistrust and marginalization of single people within the community of faith is inconsistent with the teaching of Scripture and is more reflective of the idolatry of the world.

In the spirit of the evangelical strategy of assimilation, I grew up in the era of the attractional church model and commercial Christian evangelicalism. The Christian book and music industry experienced tremendous growth during my coming-of-age years in the late 1990s and early 2000s. Modern worship music, which attempted to mimic the concert scene, began to supersede traditional sanctuary worship. Bestselling evangelical purity culture books, such as Joshua Harris's *I Kissed Dating Goodbye*, dominated the church youth group scene.[38] The messages came at us fast, through multiple kinds of media, giving us little time to critically examine the soundness of the theology they presented. Upon reflection as an adult, I have been able to summarize the main points of the

---

[38] In recent years Harris has announced his identification as an exvangelical (ex-evangelical) and publicly apologized for the harmful ideas his writing peddled and perpetuated.

60

marriage theology and its subtext that I inherited from the church and the Christian purity culture of the 1990s and 2000s.

1. **Every good Christian (and normal person) marries.** Singleness is weird and is not a viable option for holy living. One of the most important things young people can do to prepare for successful lives is learn how to be godly husbands and wives. The sooner you find Mr. or Ms. Right, the more blessed you are. (One of the worst tragedies of life would be becoming an old maid or bachelor.)

2. **Sex within marriage is sacred, amazing, gratifying, and beautiful.** Many Christian leaders in my experience spoke of married sex as holy, almost divine. Your sex life will be automatically blessed and incredibly satisfying if you choose a Christian spouse and save sex until marriage. Sex outside of Christian marriage is dirty and horribly sinful. The only difference between horribly sinful sex and divine, eternally gratifying sex was heterosexual Christian marriage.

3. **A marriage with Jesus at its center will lead to lifelong fulfillment.** Note that *marriage*, not *Jesus*, is the subject of that sentence. The reason "other people's" marriages fail is that they didn't put Jesus at the center. Having a great marriage is one of the best ways to witness to the outside world.

Other people whose marriages are doomed to fail will want the kind of marriage you have, which will lead them to Christ.

I hope that the church, in your experience, communicated more helpful messages about sex and marriage to you than it did to me. I hope the marriage theology you've been taught was more biblical and less commercially Christian. I hope you were better than I was at filtering subtle, perhaps unintended messages and interpreting them in a more helpful way. It has taken several years of my adult life for me to deconstruct these false messages and mitigate the harm they have caused in my own life and theology. Sadly, as much as I wanted my weddings to be a testimony to my faith in God, my personal marriages did not end up being a positive mirroring of Christ and the church to the world. Instead, I have discovered God's powerful grace in my experience of physically and emotionally surviving the two marriages I thought were within the will of God. It is easier for me than for many to confess that marriage and romantic love have definitely not been my personal savior.

The church's witness should prophetically declare that romantic love does not save people from unhappy lives but that Jesus does! The church should proclaim that everything we need is not wrapped up in a romantic partner but is found in Jesus! The church should preach that our identity, our drive, our life, our soul are not found in a human soul mate but in Jesus, the lover of souls! When the church publicly fails to put romantic relationships in proper perspective to a relationship with Jesus, *and* when the church is the iconic place for weddings, it is easy to lead the world into confusion. However unlikely it may be, one bold and prophetic way to clarify the church's true object of worship might be for the church to stop holding celebrations of romantic love under the guise of worship services, or at least stop expecting/requiring clergy to lead them. Even in the most well-intentioned wedding ceremonies, it is difficult to overcome the prevailing cultural idol of the divinization of romantic love.

## Chapter 6

# Where Do We Go from Here?

The current theology of marriage in the church is not just *not* supported by Scripture, tradition, reason, and experience, it has actually wounded hundreds of thousands of people. It is one of the great harms we have done to the world that the emerging church will have to seek to heal. Considering the resources we have in Scripture, tradition, reason, and experience, it is worth seriously reevaluating the church's prominent involvement in this multi-billion-dollar marriage business in the United States. The church's involvement has undeniably provided cherished memories for many couples, but it has also been divisive. According to Jesus, "no city or house divided against itself will stand" (Matt. 12:25; see also Mark 3:25; Luke 11:17), so perhaps it would do us some good to decentralize the thing that's dividing us, both in our theological emphasis as well as in our practice. Changing human behavior and centuries of tradition is certainly easier said than done. The practical details would be a challenge that a creative and Spirit-filled team would have to discuss. I can only share some of my own imagination.

I do not advocate for strict return to biblical wedding practices, particularly as it relates to patriarchal norms. The advances made in gender equality over the centuries are evidence of the teachings of Jesus improving and elevating the status of women. These gains are too important to lose. But what about the clergy role in weddings? Perhaps that aspect of ancient wedding practice is worth reviving. Wedding ceremonies could be better suited once again as private affairs directed by the couples and their families and friends. Perhaps a well-spoken, supportive friend or family member could fulfill the legal role required for solemnization. This trend is already gaining in popularity among emerging generations. Another option would be to allow a judge to fulfill the role of the agent of the state and then celebrate together with family, friends, and supportive community.

There could be something really useful in returning power to the couple and their families, where it belongs. Without clergypersons involved in an official capacity of sanctioning or solemnizing, perhaps couples themselves would take more personal responsibility for their choices in pairing.

The decisions to marry and whom to marry are deeply personal. They involve issues of self-worth, compatibility, sexual orientation, gender, finance, life goals, family cultures, expectations, child-rearing, housing, lifestyles, personal habits, and so much more. The decisions to marry and whom to marry also impact the social systems of families and local communities. At the end of the day, each of us will only be responsible for the consequences of our own relationships and decisions and how they affected us and the world around us. There is something empowering about returning ultimate responsibility to the couple themselves and reminding them of their important role in owning their decision-making.

Perhaps clergy members could return to a role of biblical counsel and blessing, even if this work is more time-consuming, more private, and not as financially profitable. If pastors were to take the role of counsel seriously, perhaps seminaries and other centers for pastoral training would offer more suitable preparation for this important and biblical support role. Perhaps pastors truly could provide support for each couple to have the healthiest, most life-giving, Christ-honoring relationship possible. At the very least, perhaps denominational rules should allow for clergypersons to decide for themselves whether their own pastoral role need include the solemnization of weddings.

What about location? Even though couples can choose to have a wedding ceremony in many offsite locations, destinations, or homes, some may still desire to wed in a church. Perhaps the church could decide to rent its space to private parties for wedding nuptials, much like a family birthday party or family reunion, without the involvement of clergy. Such churches may additionally want to consider whether space rental should include a worship sanctuary or utilize areas instead like a fellowship hall or gymnasium. In such cases, the church would do well to offer this venue equitably. When considering prices, churches should be sensitive to socio-economic factors. Some off-site venues cost more than others, and affordable use of space within a church can sometimes alleviate a financial burden for financially hurting families. A more radical choice would be for a church to reclaim its worship space solely for the worship of God and refuse to host weddings in the worship space at all. There are certainly many other lovely wedding venues out there. In any case, the current discrimination of some churches to provide services for heterosexual but not homosexual couples can be extremely painful. Whatever the church decides, whether renting space out to private parties or providing counsel, a policy of nondiscrimination could help provide a more safe and loving community.

Marriage can provide humanity with a special kind of companionship that includes sexual enjoyment, love, comfort, reproduction, and support. But marriage—or "true love"— shouldn't be the ultimate goal of a follower of Christ. Even Jesus admits that marriage is not eternal. In the age to come, people will not be marrying (see Matt. 22:30; Mark 12:25). All of us regardless of sexual orientation will lay aside our sexuality in the age to come. The purpose of marriage on this earth at this time is mainly to serve as an optional resource to help us navigate our human lives. In and of themselves, neither sex nor marriage is holy or divine in any way. Something becomes holy only when God touches it. In this sense, matrimony certainly *can* be holy. But so can many other common life events and experiences—such as adopting a child, moving into a new home, enjoying a meal with a good friend, experiencing God in nature, getting a job promotion, or praying with someone in a hospital room. The church does not, as a rule, require a clerical presence or plan worship services to celebrate these other types of sacred life events or decisions. By the grace of God, holy experiences and relationships fill our lives. Matrimony can be holy. But we need to guard ourselves against elevating matrimony to a higher position than it deserves. Only the Lord is holy, holy, holy.

# BIBLIOGRAPHY

Anderson, David. "Before God and These Witnesses: An Evangelistic Guide to Weddings." PhD diss., Liberty University, 2017.

Binder Kadden Barbara. "Jewish Weddings: When and Where They Happen." *My Jewish Learning*. Accessed December 3, 2021. https://www.myjewishlearning.com/article/time-place-for-a-jewish-wedding/.

Feldman, Daniel. "The Development of Minhag as a Reflection on Halakhic Values: The Pre-wedding Fast." *Tradition* 35, no. 1 (2001).

Gonzalez, Justo L. *The Story of Christianity: The Early Church to the Dawn of the Reformation.* New York: HarperOne, 2010.

IBISWorld. "Wedding Services in the U.S.: Market Size 2005–2027," updated April 29, 2021, https://www.ibisworld.com/industry-statistics/market-size/wedding-services-united-states/.

Jones, Jeffrey. "U.S. Church Membership Falls Below Majority for First Time." Gallup, March 29, 2021. https://news.gallup.com/poll/341963/church-membership-falls-below-majority-first-time.aspx.

Knueven, Liz. "The Average Wedding Cost $19,000 in 2020, about $10,000 Less Than the Year Before." *Business Insider*, June 3, 2021. https://www.businessinsider .com/personal-finance/how-much-does-a-wedding-cost.

Lamm, Maurice. "The Location of a Jewish Wedding." Chabad-Lubavitch Media Center. https://www.chabad.org /library/article_cdo/aid/480509/jewish/The-Location-of -a-Jewish-Wedding.htm.

Lipka, Michael. "Mainline Protestants Make up Shrinking Number of U.S. Adults." Pew Research Center, May 18, 2015. https://www.pewresearch.org/fact-tank/2015 /05/18/mainline-protestants-make-up-shrinking-number -of-u-s-adults/.

Millard, Egan. "2019 Parochial Reports Show Continued Decline and a 'Dire' Future for the Episcopal Church." Episcopal News Service, October 16, 2020. https://www.episcopalnewsservice.org/2020/10/16/2019 -parochial-reports-show-continued-decline-and-a-dire-future-for-the-episcopal-church/.

Phillips, Beth. "1 Corinthians 7 and Singleness in the Church." *Leaven*, Vol. 9, Iss. 3, Article 4, 2001. https:// digitalcommons.pepperdine.edu/leaven/vol9/iss3/4 .

Ponzetti, James J. and Barbara Horkoff Mutch. "Marriage as Covenant: Tradition as a Guide to Marriage Education in the Pastoral Context." *Pastoral Psychology* 54, no. 3 (2006).

# Bibliography

Presbyterian Church USA. "Summaries of Statistics, Comparative Summaries." Pcusa.org.

Revised Statues of Missouri, XXX Stat. 451.100 (1998), https://www.mo.gov/home-family/marriage-divorce/.

Ritzer, Korbinian. *Formen, Riten, und Religiöses Brauchtum der Eheschliessung in den Christlichen Kirchen des Ersten Jahrtausends.* Münster: Aschendorff, 1962.

Scanlon, Leslie. "PC(USA) Releases 2020 Statistical Report." *The Presbyterian Outlook.* April 22, 2021. https://pres -outlook.org/2021/04/pcusa-releases-2020-statistical -report/.

Stevenson, Kenneth. *Nuptial Blessing: A Study of Christian Marriage Rites.* New York: Oxford University Press, 1983.

Stocquart, Emile. "Marriage in Roman Law." *Yale Law Journal* 16, 1907.

Roberts, Alexander, and James Donaldson, eds. *The Ante-Nicene Fathers.* 1885-1887. 10 vols. Repr., Peabody, MA: Hendrickson, 1994.

*The Book of Discipline of the United Methodist Church: 2016.* Nashville: United Methodist Publishing House, 2016.